Man Cave Devotions

Your Relationships Matter

Compiled by:

CJ Willis

RELENTLESS
PUBLISHING

Co-Authors

Napoleon Bradford

Andre Gilliard

Cornell Jones

Trimanie McFadden

Samuel Summers

CJ Willis

Ronald Willis

Man Cave Devotions, Volume 1 : Your Relationships Matter

Published by :

Relentless Publishing House, LLC

www.relentlesspublishing.com

RELENTLESS
PUBLISHING

ISBN: 9781948829441

Volume 1: June 2020

Dedication

This book is dedicated to every man who felt like his voice didn't matter. Be encouraged and stay strong. We see you. We hear you. We need you. Keep talking!

CONTENTS

Foreword

It has been said for years that "the man" is the head of the family! This seems to be one of the most common cliché's that exist. While it sounds "good on paper", this statement could not be further from the truth in theory. The head of something is the top or the summit, the starting point, the center. Man is not and will never be the starting point of the family. Why? Because God is! The institution of family began with God. God is the original father and the progenitor of the family. He had the first son! He is the starting point, He is the head!

So if man is not "head of the family" then what is he? I can tell you what he is, man is the bottom! As men, we are called to be "the foundation" of the family. WE ARE THE BOTTOM!

We are the building grounds that God uses to establish the construction of the family on. When you are constructing a building, the most important and the most expensive task is always the "pouring of the foundation". If you get this step wrong, the whole project will be wrong.

In this book, Man Cave Devotions, Volume 1: Your Relationships Matter, you will get a wealth of information, insight and perspectives on one of the most important foundational characteristics that a man must possess-the ability to relate! This collection will provide you with wisdom on a man's relationship in three keys areas, his relationship with God, his relationship with Family/Friends, and his relationship with Money! The insight for each of these authors serves as a "buffet" for the man looking to gain wisdom in these areas.

In a time where real men are a dying breed, it is refreshing for us to be able to get back to the "cave" and put the focus back on strengthening the foundation of the family-MEN! We need more men that can relate on a higher level. Why? Because every building is only as strong and as valuable as it's foundation!

Rudeco Roberts
Change agent, Speaker and Founder
The Kingdom Management Group

We are a sum total
of what we have
learned from all
who have taught us,
both great and
small.

-Dr. Myles Munroe

Man's Relationship with God

Beginning The Walk

Your intimacy with God starts with your prayer life. It will not be like the prayers you hear in church. It probably won't be pretty or what people call deep. God is not interested in all that. He's interested in it being true. If you keep it 100 with God, that's what He wants. Talk to God like you would talk to your boy in good and bad times. This is where your ego and pride goes out the door. You may have to do it alone at first. Don't worry if the words don't all fit or even make sense. You may be surprised but God understands street lingo too. Most people equate prayer with just talking to God but He does not want a one-sided conversation. He's interested in a dialogue, which means a two-way conversation. You talk He listens. He talks you listen. Like all fathers, it does not mean you get an instantaneous response but like all true fathers, He's working to fix your problems and advise you on the right moves to make. For those of you who may not have grown up with a father, this may be a new experience but you will get use to it. Just be patient and take it easy.

-CJ Willis

Don't Be Fake

The fundamental nature of our survival requires humanity to be in a relationship. However, many people neglect the most crucial relationship, and that is the one with God. This neglect consists of many reasons. However, I think the most disturbing reason is a focus on religion versus having a relationship with God. Although some religious aspect is necessary, it is a relationship with God that creates authenticity toward being obedient to his word. Religion is an outward expression of complying with the Bible without establishing a connection with God. Simply put, without the connection, it is a fake.

Complying with the Bible is good, but it does not create belief, it creates compliance. Therefore, compliance along is not enough. It must be accompanied with belief, which creates obedience. In other words, we are not merely trying to comply with the Bible but be obedient to it. Obedience comes from our relationship with God, but we must first have an intimate relationship with him. The word intimate sounds wrong if you are a man, and especially if it does not involve sex. Contrary to men, most women want an intimate relationship outside of sex. Intimacy requires vulnerability, which is often viewed by men as being weak, wearing your emotions on your sleeve, or a lack of masculinity. Conversely, being vulnerable is what connects us to God and each other. It draws us nearer to God and people, creating a more profound connection that can only be found in being vulnerable. Without it, there is no connection, and we are only practicing religion.

Vulnerability reveals our entire identity, not only to include our strengths, but our weakness, imperfections, and fears. It opens our hearts to receive Christ while allowing him to reside internally with us. He knows you by what is in your heart and not by your actions and talk. Actions sometimes are deceptive, and talk is not always truthful. The heart does not lie. Real strength is being vulnerable while denying vulnerability is running away from your true self, and that is a sign of weakness. Men do not be afraid to be vulnerable, for God did not give us a spirit of fear, but of power, love, and a sound mind (2 Timothy 1:7, NKJV). God requires vulnerability to have an intimate relationship with him.

Religion without a relationship is a fake and it hinders your relationship with God creating invulnerable while lacking intimacy.

-Ronald Willis

God and Man

My advice to another man who is struggling with their walk with God. Is to know that God will never leave you nor forsake you. Don't give up on your faith. At the end of the day, your faith is all you have. Faith is the only way to have a relationship with God. Sometimes your faith will be tested. And without faith it is impossible to please God. Hebrews 11:6

My personal encounter with God began when I was a teenager. As a child I grew up in a single parent home, due to my father passing away when I was two- years old, while watching my mother struggle to raise me and five of my siblings. My mother worked two-part- time jobs which left my two older siblings to tend to the younger siblings and take care of the home. At the tender age of two, I was too young to understand why my father wasn't in my life. As I grew to become a teenager; I attended church with my mother. She instilled godly values in my life. Even though I obeyed my mother and attended church without acting out, I secretly was angered with God because I felt he took my father too soon. I never got a chance to know my father. I never had the chance to go fishing with him or have him teach me how to ride a bike.

My relationship with God struggled at times as well. As I grew into manhood, I continued to attend church. It was at that point in my life, I realized it wasn't God's fault my father passed, but that it was God's will.

As my relationship grew I learned that God was there with me as a teenager and that he was my Heavenly Father. He was watching over me all those years.

What is man, that thou art mindful of him? And the son of man, that thou visit him.
Psalm 8:4

-Cornell Jones

Lord, Save Me From Me

As men, we are often exposed to situations that tend to cause us to be forced to make decisions that have a lasting impact on our future. These decisions often come as a result of ideologies that stem from our formation. In other words, based on who raised us, poured into us, modeled behavior for us, or celebrated our accomplishments, we formulated ideas about what was right and what was wrong. We often reproduced the behaviors that provided us with either positive affirmation or experiences in the past, even when those behaviors are not correct.

Paul, in his letter to the church at Rome, articulates this decision-making process as a wrestle between the SPIRIT and the flesh, or the law and the flesh, where the SPIRIT or Law represents what is right, and the flesh representing what is wrong. Based on Paul's synopsis, these opponents are a part of the same being, and this suggests that with every decision, every thought, every action, there are equally-powerful yet opposing forces fighting to get us to yield to their "will". Paul says it like this in Romans 7:19, "For the good that I will to do, I do not do; but the evil I will not to do, that I practice." He goes on to write in Romans 7:22, "For I delight in the law of GOD according to the inward man. But I see another law in my members, warring against the law of my mind, and bringing me into captivity to the law of sin which is in my members."

As men, we must begin to provide deliberate clarity as to which of these opposing views we will heed, but we can't do it by ourselves. Paul likens this awkward warring within his members as a "body of death." But there is an answer, and that answer comes from including JESUS CHRIST into your decision-making process. In other words, instead of trying to make the decision on your own, simply pause and pray, and allow JESUS to be the deciding factor of the decisions you make.

-Napoleon Bradford

Divine Encounter

Your relationship with The Most High God (Jesus) is the most important relationship you will ever have. It sets the tone for all others. Building a relationship with God is like other interactions with people, you plan time to spend together, you speak back and forth to one another, but where it differs at first is He speaks to you through the word of God, The Bible. You speak to Him through prayer. He doesn't always answer prayers quickly or the way you want but never doubt He always answers.

As you get to know Him through the word, you obtain great wisdom, understanding and love for Him. You also learn how His love for you is beyond measure. The wisdom and understanding you obtain increases your inner strength, love for others, yourself and your dependence on Him. Why dependence on Him? God created all things on heaven and earth. He knows all, sees all, is everywhere and loves all.

Who else has this power in life and is willing to take time with you daily to teach you life principals if you desire? As you begin to shed the chains of fear, insecurity, greed and malice and put on righteous, the man you become starts to be noticed by others. You become more trusted, respected, valued and your finances may even increase, but these strong attributes are not just for you but were built in you to serve others as well. You then achieve peace within yourself through this honest and obedient relationship with God, something no other man, woman or material possession on earth can give you. It surpasses all understanding and knowledge. All these characteristics continue to grow within you for the rest of your life and this relationship unlikely any other on earth will continue forever.

-Andre Gillard

In His Image

My youngest child is a Michael Jackson fanatic....and he's only ten! For hours, he watches any and everything Michael Jackson. Live performances, music videos, biographical films, the Pepsi commercials and of course The Wiz. He practically knows all lyrics to every Michael Jackson song and the best part is seeing him imitate the King of Pop's dance moves. He often does this while looking at himself in the mirror. Curious to know which song was his favorite, surprisingly, out of the 10 released studio albums, over 90 recorded songs and 10 number one hits my son's favorite is Man in the Mirror. When I asked why, my son explains "..... this is why I can dance just like him Dad, because this song encourages me to look in the mirror while I dance to make sure I do the moves just like him."

That Boy Acts Just Like His Dad

When the crowds saw what Paul had done, they raised their voice, saying in the Lycaonian language, "The gods have become like men and have come down to us."

Acts 14:11

It was in Lystra, after fleeing the city of Iconium from an attempt on his life, where Paul continued to preach and encountered a man, crippled from birth, who never walked a day in his life. As Paul preached, he noticed the faith of the crippled man and commanded the man to "Stand upright on your feet." The man immediately sprang up and began walking.

Paul, being an eyewitness to the miracles of Jesus could now also perform a miracle himself. But how could Paul do such a thing. John 20:29 reads: Jesus saying, "Because you have seen Me, you have believed; blessed are those who have not seen and yet believed." Paul was there. He watched Jesus perform miracles time and time again. See his belief and faith in Christ allowed him to now act like and imitate his Savior. And so it is with us today, through our belief and relationship with Christ, we too hold the possibility and potential to pray and declare the miraculous.

Men! We should often stand in the mirror and take a self-assessment and ask ourselves... Who am I imitating? Do my ways, thoughts, and actions reflect that of God's Image? Is my life the way I am living right now pleasing to God? Can others see God in ME?

And God said, Let us make man in our image, after our likeness: and let them have dominion....

Genesis 1:26-28 KJV

-Trimanie McFadden

Man's Relationship with Money

Stewardship

You can conquer your money. It's called
stewardship, and the Bible often teaches
about it. When it comes to your money,
you're going to have to decide what is your long
term will and goals for your life and the finances
you need for your life to be what you want it to be.
The discipline it takes to serve God, run a family,
or own a business is the same discipline it takes to
manage your money. Your relationship with
money is a tale, not of your financial prowess, but
of your financial, spiritual, or mental discipline.

What does that mean? That means having your
money in order so that you can use it as a tool to
provide for yourself first, your family and be able
to be a generous giver to God. This means you first
have to develop self-discipline, which is based in
self-denial. For example, if you want a beautiful
home with a wife and children, all of that will be

affected by your money. If you want your children to not live in abject poverty, that will be affected by your money.

You don't start managing your money when you get these things, you start managing your money before you get these things. You start saving for when there's no reason to save and planning when there's no reason to plan. The man that waits until disaster is upon him to make decisions, is always reacting to the environment instead of controlling his environment.

A man of wisdom, on the other hand, prepares for situations and circumstances ahead of time. The first suggestion in financial preparation is making an obtainable budget based on present income and adjusting your lifestyle to it. The second suggestion is to truly cut unnecessary expenditures. For example, do you need to go out all weekend long? The third suggestion is to start a modest savings account. For example, save $5 a month. Fellows I know you're not going to like the last suggestion and say it's a girl thing but it works. The fourth and final suggestion is learning to use coupons. Coupon money is fun money. The more money you save with coupons, the more money you have to have fun.

PS: I go grocery shopping at 2:30 in the morning and use self-checkout.

-CJ Willis

The True Measure of
Success Is Love

Mans greatest accomplishment is not found through being financially successful but through his ability to love. Scriptures explain, that although we may speak in different languages, have the gift of prophecy, have knowledge, but we gained nothing if we do not have love (1 Corinthians 13, 1-3, NIV).

Men normally focuses on being financially successful, and rightfully, so, they are usually considered the provider. Although this is admirable, it does nothing without love. Love is the bond that brings us together, and it is the true measure of success. Everyone will not be financially successful, but everyone can love.

However, love is often overlooked and underused, resulting in millions of broken homes. We all need and want love. However, initially we solely depend on our parents at birth to give us love, and if they do not, then what. I was a victim of then what. My grandmother raised me, but I desperately wanted my parent's love. This desire created empty feelings that haunted me throughout my childhood, creating the pain of feeling abandoned while also having suicidal ideation, low self-esteem, and social anxiety.

After becoming an adult, I ventured out to seek love. However, my efforts resulted into several failed marriages. Conversely, I discovered the love that I was seeking is not found in people, but through a relationship with God. This is not to suggest that people do not have love, but it is to understand that love comes from God (1 John 4, 7 NIV).

God's love empowered me to love myself, but it also changed my direction to look for someone to love versus looking for someone to love me. Love is a continuous cycle that is not designed for us to merely received it, but also give it.

Babies focus on receiving love, but men focus on giving love. Scripture explains, when I became a man, I put the ways of childhood behind me (1 Corinthians 13, 12 NIV). In other words, it is childish to only receive love. Love comes from our relationship with God, who provides us with the true measure of success.

-Ronald Willis

Back To The Basics

One of the most confusing areas that man has to deal with and develop in is finances. How men handle money is often not discussed directly but is subliminally taught through the images and lessons we observe growing up. Rarely did we see positive images of saving, and wealth creation, for more often we saw those who were struggling, barely able to pay their bills, or we saw those who squandered their resources in extravagant material acquisitions. We saw people who wore jewelry and put rims on their car, but lived with their parents or in raggedy rented dwellings.

With all of those mixed messages and images, where does one go to really learn about GOD's expectation of man with money? Well most would say the Bible, and would probably direct you to Old Testament passages about tithing or New Testament passages about sowing and reaping. I believe to find out GOD's expectations of man and money, we must go to the first instruction GOD gives man. Genesis 1:28, after GOD formed man and woman and blessed them, GOD gives man five commands that I believe are still essential lessons for managing money and manhood.

First, GOD says, "Be fruitful." GOD tells man to get a job. Then GOD says, "Multiply." GOD tells man to invest so that the value of what is earned increases. Next GOD says, "Fill the Earth." GOD tells man to acquire property and have such an integrous life that it covers his space with positivity. Then GOD says, "Subdue it." GOD tells man to bring his affairs under submission to him. That means to pay bills on time and not get in debt or get in agreements that cannot be fulfilled. Finally, GOD says, "Have dominion." GOD tells man that after he has gotten all those areas together, he must take complete control so that he is never controlled by any item other than GOD. In other words, as long as we have dominion over things, they never become our idols, and never get in the way of our GOD given purpose.

-Napoleon Bradford

Who's The Master

We see and hear of where the love of money has crushed hundreds of thousands of relationships. It has broken up marriages. It is the #1 reason for divorce and family crisis ahead of infidelity in this country. Yet with this information and knowledge widely known we continuously fall into the same deception. For many men, money is the most important thing in their life, whether they realize it or not. It empowers them with a false sense of self-confidence, boldness and brings them praise, popularity and even worship. They believe that with enough money, they are smarter and better than those who do not have it. It is relied upon as a child who relies upon their parents. This dependence is so strong that the individual believes it can serve and satisfy ALL their needs. Some would do almost anything for money. Things such as, lie, cheat, steal and/or kill depending on the situation and who is involved. It is safe to say money is their master and they are its slave.

We come into this world with nothing and will take nothing out. Do not view money as more than an instrument obtained to gain access to goods and services for the needs and wants in our lives. Money should not be our God. It is not the place where we place our hope, trust and peace we seek. Our ethical standards should not be based on our financial prosperity or lack of. For where your treasure is, there your heart will be also (Matthew 6:21) NASB

I would like you to think on and answer the following questions with complete honestly. Once you have answered this questions I challenge you to pose them to your family and friends. They will bring clarity and truth to your life;

1. What position does money hold in your life? If is #1 then why?

2. Who are you with or without money (Character & Attitude) Do they change based on your finances

3. What is the standard for your life? (What do you live by)

4. Who and What is your faith in and Why?

-Andre Gilliard

The Almighty Dollar

S ing it with me: *Money, money, money, money, MONEY. Some people got to have it. Some people really need it. For the love of money, people will steal from their mother. People will rob their own brother. That almighty dollar.* (The O'Jays – For the Love of Money)

Let's face it. Everyone needs money. To be more specific, EVERY MAN MUST have a way to earn income in order to 'be' (i.e. perform) as a man. We all know the well-known scripture in 1 Timothy 6:10 (KJV), *"For the love of money is the root of all evil: which while some coveted after, they have erred from the faith, and pierced themselves through with."*

We tend to only focus on the first part of this scripture ignoring the deeper significance of its entirety. In fact, the Bible does not disapprove of the amassing of wealth. On the contrary, there are several scriptures that support the gathering of resources. One such example is scripture is Proverbs 13:11 which lets us know that the *"gathering (of wealth) little by little will increase it".* What is immoral is the yearn for money which drives some to improper means to gain wealth hastily.

I have several real-life examples of loved ones, close friends and associates who have made failed attempts at get-rich-quick schemes that ultimately leave them in a worse condition than their former present. Rather than making an honest income they resort to selling drugs, bank robberies, illegal pyramid schemes, and con-artist business dealings leading to years, even decades of incarceration and paying of retribution. These same individuals are now putting their lives back together again, bit by bit after losing half of their early adulthood to prison...all for the love of an earthly treasure.

Matthew 19: 16-26 lets us know that God doesn't value or require of us wealth to be perfect. Jesus tells a young man, after being asked how to have eternal life, to sell all he had and give to the poor and he will have treasure in heaven. Now, that in itself seems like a ridiculous insinuation that we, Christ-followers, should not have wealth. What it does mean is that we should strive to have a comfortable living within our means while sowing out of our 'overflow' to the building of God's Kingdom and to care for the poor. Wealth and the accumulation of such should never outweigh our desire to follow the will of Christ. When we embrace Christ, we must let go of the world, for we cannot serve God and money.

Yes, as a man, we need money to provide and support our families to have a good home and be the maintainers of our women and family and to set aside an inheritance for our children. Yet, we are also commanded to give generously to the less fortunate and to speak up on their behalf. This is the key to real wealth!

Give generously to [the poor] and do so without a grudging heart, then because of this the Lord your God will bless you in all your work and in everything you put your hand to. There will always be poor people in the land. Therefore I command you to be openhanded toward your fellow Israelites who are poor and needy in your land. —
Deuteronomy 15:10-11

-Trimanie McFadden

It's Fishing Time

One of most important topics we men must discuss is finances. We as men have always accepted the role as the "bread winner" and with that comes a responsibility. We are charged with making and managing money to provide for our family. Money gives you power. Power is the ability to make things happen. Sometimes some people abuse that power. Make the money,but do not let the money make or change you.

When the dust settles it all boils down to sacrifices and choices. We all have the same 24 hours in a day. What we are doing within those 24 hours? People without financial literacy must do two things, either get educated or hit rock bottom. That is where the change begins. We must teach our family and friends the importance of saving, investing, and budgeting. It is like the saying "give a man a fish and you feed him for a day; teach a man to fish and you feed him for a lifetime." That makes them less of a burden on you. We must remember some people were never taught certain things. Take the time to reach back and lift as you climb to financial stability and wealth.

1 Timothy 6:10

"For the love of money is a root of all kinds of evil. Some people, eager for money, have wandered from the faith and pierced themselves with many griefs."

-Samuel Summers

Man's Relationship with Family & Friends

Growing Up Was Tough

G rowing up' was tough! I was the youngest of three brothers; raised in a single parent home. My father was absent. He, along with countless others fell victim to the crack cocaine epidemic that rocked the black communities in the mid-1980s. Before addiction, my father was a great provider and maintainer of his home and handled his responsibilities with pride. Going out of his way to do anything for anyone in need was second nature to dad. A possessor of many talents and natural abilities, my father was a skilled craftsman, a carpenter, auto-mechanic, an artist, a singer, a praying man, the neighborhood barber, and life of any party. Honorable, hard-working, integrity, loving, and being a man's man are just a few of the attributes that comes to mind when I think of him in my youth. My parents required of us attendance and participation in church and provided examples by serving in church in various capacities themselves.

My father instilled in my brothers and I the need to be strong, educated, and disciplined from an early childhood. "You gotta be tough kid..." is one if his often-repeated sayings. After addiction however, my father's presence took a gradual descent into obscurity. 'Payday Fridays' eventually became weekends of full of "Mom, is dad coming home" questions. The financial support deteriorated so using the toughness instilled by dad, my brothers and I started working early on to lend a hand to support mom and each other. And we live by this courage to this day.

Now I am all 'GROWN UP'! Married with children of my own. As I reminisce, Proverbs 22:6 comes to mine, which reads: "Train up a child in the way he should go: and when he is old, he will not depart from it." Although my father's ability to provide monetary and emotional support to his family may have been repressed, the lessons learned through his personal struggles I will cherish and carry with me forever. Those lessons taught me to accept my own personal responsibilities as a man...as a husband....and as a father which are: to provide for, to protect, to love, and to lead!

And to this day, I spend as much time and energy as a dad to make sure every moment we still have together is filled with laughter, respect and love. As a man, I chose not to hold grudges and forgive......for I have made the choice to not deny my faith and remain a believer and BE a provider to my relatives, especially for members of my household.

In a strange way, dad gave what he could. And what he did give, has lasted a lifetime.

But if anyone does not provide for his relatives, and especially for members of his household, he has denied the faith and is worse than an unbeliever

1 Timothy 5:8

-Trimanie McFadden

All Brothers Aren't Blood

F or so long we were taught to believe the saying, "Blood is thicker than water," or we were told, "While you can choose your friends, you can't choose your family." Both of these statements suggest that there is a preordination attached to the idea of family that makes it a primary relationship that is supreme to all other relationships. In other words, because of the blood connection, one is predisposed to forsake all other relationships for the purpose of aiding or assisting those connected by blood.

While blood relationships are important and they are out of the control of the persons connected by blood, I would also like to suggest that there are some relationships created outside of the confines of DNA that are just as powerful and just as important as actual blood relations. These relationships are forged in the classroom, in the neighborhood, on the basketball court, on the football field, or just through the matriculation and maturation of life.

A perfect example of this is the relationship between a young shepherd boy by the name of David and the son of a king by the name of Jonathan. While their backgrounds and pedigree suggested that they had no business being friends, 1 Samuel 18:1 tells us, "...the soul of Jonathan was knit to the soul of David, and Jonathan loved him as his own soul." This is immediately after David was overlooked by his father and rejected by his brothers, yet he found a connection with his friendship to Jonathan. In fact, the original Hebrew language says, "the life of Jonathan was bound up by the life for David." They were tied in such a way that was inseparable. To push it further, verse three says, "Then Jonathan and David made a covenant because he loved him as his own soul." In other words, they became brothers connected without blood.

We must be open to having friendships that are sacred, special, and solid, even if these relationships are not connected through biological blood. Brotherhood, true brotherhood, is achieved through a Spiritual Blood connection.

-Napoleon Bradford

The Husband's Role

The head of the family is the husband and wife. This nucleus will decide the atmosphere of their home, whether it is full of love or full of war. Although both husband and wife are the head, it starts with the husband knowing his role as it relates to his wife. Wives are a gift from God design for the husband to cherished, honored, bestowed, and place their needs first. She was fashioned from the man's rib (Genesis 2: 22, NIV) and made for him to serve her because she came from him. Adam said she is bone of my bone and flesh of my flesh (Genesis 2:23, NIV). Her needs are placed before the husband, before the parents, and she is placed before the children. Scripture explains that a man is to leave his parents and be united with his wife becoming one flesh (Genesis 2: 24 NIV).

The man leaves his parents and transfer his loyalty and commitment from his parents to his wife, making her first in his life outside of God. Generally, speaking, women more than men want to feel love, and placing her needs first creates this feeling. Conversely, many husbands failed to put their wives' needs first because they mistakenly attempt to control the relationship confusing that with leadership while thinking she is subordinate. Some will refer to the Bible, stating that man came before woman, therefore, that makes him superior and makes her inferior. This is ridiculous and illogical because the same thing can be said about animals, but they are not superior, although they came first.

God charged the man to leave his parents, to cleave to his wife and love her as Christ loves the Church. It is critical to understand the man is charged with doing these things and not the woman. This is not to suggest the woman is not going to do the same. God knows if the man does his part according to God's will, the woman will do the same. The man must understand these roles are purposefully design by God to leave, cleave, and love her according to God's will. The man will need to surrender his selfish desire allowing God to guide and direct his heart. Husbands that understand their role in their marriage according to God's word will have a home full of love and not war. They will serve their wives creating a strong bond full of love. Her sexuality and her beauty demands it. The love between the husband and wife is the greatest gift children can receive from their parents.

-Ronald Willis

Family Values

Family relationships can be the most complicated out of all relationships. Some people feel family is the most important thing in the world. Some others may not like or even enjoy being around family members. They may have bad attitudes, think they are better than you, selfish, materialistic, and/or lazy. But then the question also is how do they see you? You did not choose them they were chosen for you, born into it.

You may suffer for them, because of them, and with them. Some even feel they were born into the wrong family because their personal ideas and philosophies are very different from the ones of their immediate family or entire family structure. You hear things like don't give up on them, don't turn your back on them, look after them and always forgive them. Regardless of what most of us think about each other, we all have some of the same problems, goals, desires, needs, insecurities, and fears. Everyone in the world is looking for two things, *Value* and *Love*.

We want to be valued and loved for who we are, our ideas, work ethic, mindset, cooking, etc. We are looking for self-worth and strong purpose for our lives. You may disagree but look at all those family members that have serious issues and what happened in their lives and what they do daily. Do they show or live as if they are valued? Do they have self-confidence? Do they have a strong purpose? This includes your wife and kids if you have them. If we do not get value from our family, then we go looking for it elsewhere and this is where most issues begin.

Family is where our foundation should be built, and the foundation should be deep and strong. It is the community where we hone our personality, character, strengthened morally and principals defined and grown. Loved unconditionally, disciplined, and a place you can return when the world beats you up. Family should be a community of loved ones, making great memories, bearing each others burdens, uplifting the broken and brokenhearted. Most do not have a family that fits this description. Sometimes you must become the change you want to see. Oh, and yes this requires sacrifice, but what great endeavor does not. Relationship are about love. Family is about acceptance.

-Andre Gilliard

Building
Relationships Are
Important

Growing up in a single- parent home with four siblings, I was the middle child. I had to rely on my older siblings to tend to the house and take care of me. My mother taught my siblings and me, that family is important. Family should always stick together and help each other no matter what.

In my mid-twenties, I had to once again depend on my sister and her husband. I found myself unemployed and homeless. My sister asked me to move to Detroit, Michigan, where the automobile factories were hiring. I was able to obtain employment and become financially stable. It showed me that my family did stick together like my mother instilled in us. I have always tried to help my family out the best I could by providing financial help and allowing family members to live with me if needed.

There are "friends" who destroy each other, but a real friend sticks closer than a brother.

Proverbs 18:24 NLT

After staying with my sister and her husband for a year, I moved in with my best friend. We shared the bills and household responsibilities. I discovered that you can be acquainted with people, but a true friend is hard to find. A true friend is one who will lift you up when you are down. Ecclesiastes 4:9 NLT says, *"Two people are better off than one, for they can help each other succeed.*

Oftentimes it is hard for men to make friends because men don't show their true feelings. Men sometimes have an ego that gets in the way of forming friendships. Therefore, when we as men say someone is our friend, it didn't happen overnight. When I say someone is my homeboy that means that the relationship took some time to develop. Trust is the key. Your friend should be one that is your ride or die.

It is recommended that you at least have one good friend in life. Someone you can talk to and share your problems and concerns. Family and friends are both important to a man's personal development. They can both offer support in the time of need. Men don't generally ask for help so when one asks for help, he needs it.

-Cornell Jones

Friends vs. Associates

Throughout life you will meet people from all walks of life. Through school, work, business, church, hobbies, volunteer work etc. Some will become associates and some will become friends. Please know the difference.

Associates will be because what they or you do as in your job or organization that you all are mutually attached to. They are people you are connected to with certain goal or mission in mind someone who you are are usually professional with. Friends will be friends because of who and how you are, and your spirits will align and connect. Your relationship with friends will vary. Some friends will serve a certain purpose and then will slowly drift away. Other friends will stay for a lifetime. Every friend will usually bring something special to your circle of friends. They each have their individual role.

Friends are a necessity because they give different perspectives to help us navigate through life. Friends show up in times of need and can be the strength when we cannot find it. We must also reciprocate the type of friend we desire. We sometimes must teach our friends how we need to be loved and respected. Friends can sometimes become your enemy. They can become jealous.

Sometimes friends will learn you just to hurt you. While we love our friends, we must always proceed with caution. A true friend will always have your best interest at heart and push you to be great. Be mindful of the friends that do not clap when its times to congratulate you. Friendships serve purpose. We have friends to be therapeutic and have fun with. Friends come in handy when it comes to decision making. When you need things done, our friends are the center of networking.

Friends should always make you feel safe and be a place where you go to find understanding. You should not have to walk on eggshells around your friends. It should be consistent. Therefore, with that you both should be able to be vulnerable with each other. Your circle of friends usually defines the type of life you live.

Romans 12:10

"Love one another with brotherly affection. Outdo one another in showing honor."

-Samuel Summers

Meet the Authors

Napoleon Bradford

Napoleon Abram Bradford is a native of Sumter, South Carolina. He graduated from Morris College and Bowling Green State University. He returned to Sumter in 2006 to serve as the Assistant Principal at Mayewood Middle School and as a Guidance Counselor at Lakewood High School. He holds a Master of Divinity in Theology and two earned Doctor of Ministry degrees. In 2017, GOD led Pastor Bradford to launch The L.I.F.E. Center, a Cyber-Community of CHRIST Followers where he serves as Lead Shepherd. Napoleon is married to his 1st grade crush the former Karen Stacey Hilton, is the proud father of five of the greatest children ever.

Cornell Jones

Cornell is a native of Flint, Michigan. He is a father, provider of his home, and a man of God. He is a first time Author. He was inspired to become an Author and tell his story to help encourage others to never lose their hope. He is a hard worker and currently is employed in the automobile factory industry. He is a graduate of Flint Northwestern High School. He continues to seek education opportunities through his employment. When he is not working, he enjoys watching sports and Horror movies. He enjoys doing work outside the home that includes, gardening and yard work. He also enjoys cooking and grilling.

Andre Gilliard

Nevonia Andre Gilliard, known by most as Andre. He is married and have two children. Andre is a Veteran, Real Estate Agent, CASA GAL, and former Toastmasters member. He possess a passion for wisdom, knowledge and understanding.

Trimanie McFadden

Trimanie is a native of Sumter, SC and founder of Christ Community Cares, LLC, a Christ-centered community of businesses, community leaders, clergy, and concerned citizens. Diligently developing lifelong disciples and a community of Christ-followers through the application of the teachings and ministry of Christ is the mission. Trimaine is the former Lead Mentor of Generation N.O.W, an all-male youth mentoring program and is currently active in mentorship and community development programs throughout the city of Columbia, SC. By day, Trimaine serves as a Healthcare Cyber Security Subject Matter Expert (SME) with the largest healthcare system in the world where he travels extensively across the United States providing dialogue with industry leaders. Outside of his beautiful, loving wife and four children, Trimaine's second passion is for the underserved youth and lesser fortunate of his community.

Samuel Summers

S gt. Summers is from Bamberg, SC. He enlisted into the United States Air Force in 2001 as Security Forces Member and has been performing various military and law enforcement duties around the world foreign and domestic. He started instructing in February 2011 and since then has been able to train with first time shooters, competition shooters, multiple military and law enforcement agencies. He is a NRA and SLED certified weapons instructor.

CJ Willis

CJ was born in Texas and currently lives in South Carolina. He is the owner of WireMonkey LLC and has been in business for 10+ years. He started his business after being laid off as a car salesman for 20 years. He loves the outdoors and is passionate about men evolving into true manhood.

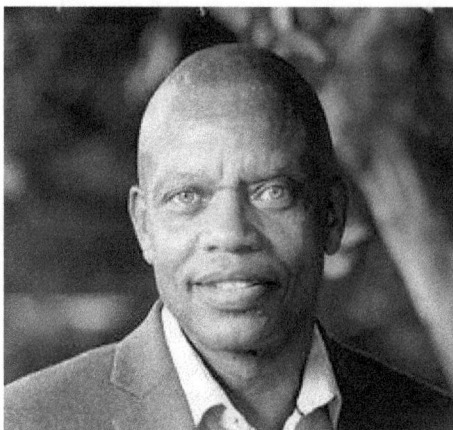

Ronald Willis

Ronald Willis was born in Glen Cove, New York, raised in Aiken, South Carolina and is currently residing in Augusta, Georgia. He recently received an honorable discharge as a Sergeant Major after serving over thirty years in the Army and Army Reserve. Ronald and his wife Charlesetta Willis have started the organization First, Focus Faith, which concentrates on spiritual, physical, mental and emotional wellness while also keeping marriages and families together as a unified body through Christ. He has a passion for teaching others about the healing power of the love of God and helping married couples have an everlasting relationship. Ronald is a proud husband, father, and grandfather of seven children and five grandchildren with one on the way.

The greatness of a man
is not in how much
wealth he acquires,
but in his integrity and
his ability to affect
those around him
positively.

–Bob Marley

www.ingramcontent.com/pod-product-compliance
Lightning Source LLC
Chambersburg PA
CBHW072211090426
42740CB00012B/2476